Author Biographies

Roald Dahl

Charlotte Guillain

Heinemann Library
Chicago, Illinois

www.capstonepub.com
Visit our website to find out more information about Heinemann-Raintree books.

To order:
☎ Phone 888-454-2279
💻 Visit www.capstonepub.com
to browse our catalog and order online.

Edited by Rebecca Rissman, Daniel Nunn, and Sian Smith
Designed by Joanna Hinton-Malivoire
Picture research by Tracy Cummins
Production by Victoria Fitzgerald
Originated by Capstone Global Library Ltd
Printed and bound in China

20 19 18 17
10 9 8 7 6

Library of Congress Cataloging-in-Publication Data
Guillain, Charlotte.
Roald Dahl / Charlotte Guillain.
p. cm.—(Author biographies)
Includes bibliographical references and index.
ISBN 978-1-4329-5962-3 (hardback)
ISBN 978-1-4329-5968-5 (paperback.)
1. Dahl, Roald—Juvenile literature. 2. Authors, English—20th century—Biography—Juvenile literature. 3. Children's stories—Authorship—Juvenile literature. I. Title.
  PR6054.A35Z68 2012
  823'.914—dc22   2011016073
  [B]

Acknowledgments
We would like to thank the following for permission to reproduce photographs: Alamy Images pp. 5 (© clive thompson people), 21 (© Greg Balfour); Corbis p. 15 (© ROBERT ERIC); Courtesy of The Roald Dahl Museum and Story Centre pp. 6, 7, 8, 10, 18 (© Roald Dahl Nominee Limited); © Disney p. 11; The Kobal Collection p. 20 (WARNER BROS/PETER MOUNTAIN); NARA p. 23g (War & Conflict CD); Penguin Group (USA) Inc. pp. 12, 13, 14, 14, 23f; Rex USA pp. 4 (ITV), 16, 17 (KENNY ELRICK); Shutterstock pp. 9 (© MAC1), 19 (© Denis Vrublevski), 23a (© crop), 23b (© Tatiana Popova), 23c (© Mark Herreid), 23d (© GFranz).

Cover image of Roald Dahl in 1983 reproduced with permission of Rex USA (Rex USA/Stephen Hyde). Back cover image of a chocolate bar with an open gold cover reproduced with permission of Shutterstock (Denis Vrublevski).

Every effort has been made to contact copyright holders of material reproduced in this book. Any omissions will be rectified in subsequent printings if notice is given to the publisher.

Disclaimer
All the Internet addresses (URLs) given in this book were valid at the time of going to press. However, due to the dynamic nature of the Internet, some addresses may have changed, or sites may have changed or ceased to exist since publication. While the author and publisher regret any inconvenience this may cause readers, no responsibility for any such changes can be accepted by either the author or the publisher.

Contents

Some words are shown in bold, **like this**. You can find them in the glossary on page 23.

Who Was Roald Dahl?

Roald Dahl was a writer.

He wrote stories for children and adults.

Roald Dahl and his books are famous all over the world.

Some of his most famous books for children are *Fantastic Mr Fox* and *Charlie and the Chocolate Factory*.

Where Did He Grow Up?

Roald Dahl was born in 1916.

He grew up in the city of Cardiff in Wales, in the United Kingdom.

Roald's mother told him stories when he was a child.

Roald wrote a diary and hid it in a tree that only he could climb.

What Did He Do Before He Was a Writer?

When Roald left school he traveled and worked in Africa.

When **World War 2** started he joined the air force and became a pilot.

Unfortunately his plane crashed and he was **injured**.

Later, he left the air force and went to work in the United States.

How Did He Start Writing Books?

In the United States, Roald wrote for a newspaper.

He wrote about his plane crash in Africa.

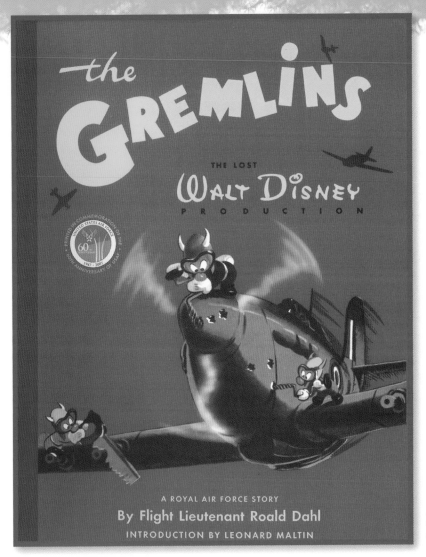

© Disney

In 1943 Roald wrote a picture book for children called *The Gremlins*.

After that he went on to write spooky stories for adults instead.

What Books Did He Write?

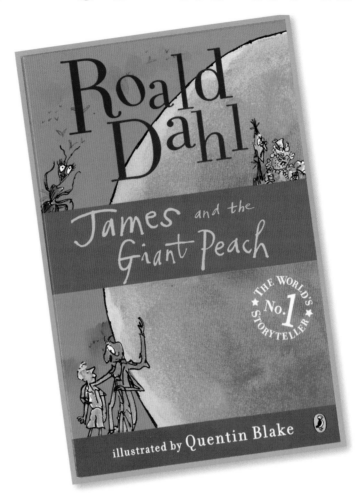

When Roald had children he started writing children's stories again.

He started by writing *James and the Giant Peach*.

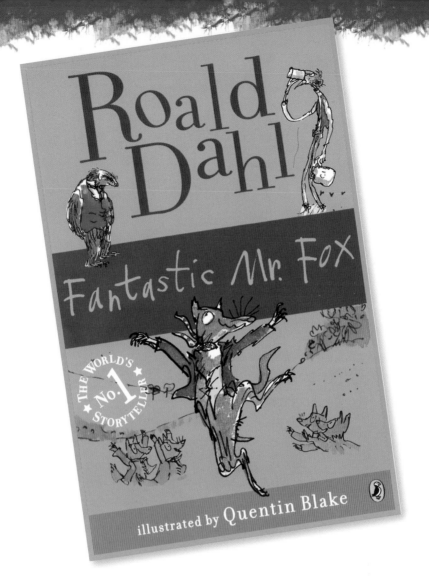

His next book was *Charlie and the Chocolate Factory*.

His other books include *Fantastic Mr Fox, The BFG, The Twits,* and *Matilda.*

What Did He Write About?

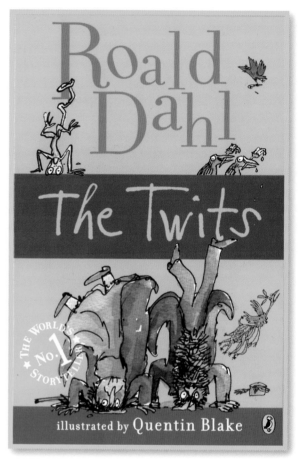

Roald often wrote about brave children who do the right thing.

There are horrible or silly adults in many of his books.

In *Matilda*, Roald wrote about a magical little girl with nasty parents.

Lots of his stories are funny, and they can be scary or wild.

Who Drew the Pictures in Roald Dahl's Books?

Quentin Blake drew the pictures for many of Roald Dahl's books.

His **illustrations** are as famous as Roald Dahl's stories.

Quentin Blake's pictures are scribbly and funny.

He draws the outline with pen and ink, then adds color with **watercolor** paint.

What Else Did Roald Like to Do?

Roald liked to grow **orchids** and other beautiful flowers.

He also bought paintings by famous artists.

He loved eating chocolate and collected the shiny wrappers.

He also visited sick children in the hospital.

Why Is He Famous Today?

Millions of children read and love Roald Dahl's books today.

People have made many movies, plays, and cartoons about his books.

Roald Dahl's **characters** are on many toys and games.

There are museums where you can find out more about Roald Dahl and his books.

Timeline of Roald Dahl's Life and Work

1916   Roald Dahl was born in Cardiff, Wales.

1939   **World War 2** started.

1940   Roald Dahl's plane crashed in Egypt.

1942   He moved to the United States.

1943   His first book, *The Gremlins*, was **published**.

1961   *James and the Giant Peach* was published.

1990   Roald Dahl died.

Glossary

 **character** person or animal in a story

 **illustration** picture that goes with a story

 **injured** hurt

 **orchid** type of plant with brightly colored flowers

 **published** made into a book or put in a magazine and printed

 **watercolor** type of paint

 **World War 2** big war that lasted for six years

Find Out More

Books

Some of Roald Dahl's books: *James and the Giant Peach, Charlie and the Chocolate Factory, Fantastic Mr Fox, The BFG, The Twits, The Witches,* and *Matilda.*

Websites

http://www.roalddahl.com/
Visit the Roald Dahl website to find out more about his life and books, look at photographs, and listen to an interview with the writer.

http://www.roalddahlmuseum.org/
If you can go to the Roald Dahl Museum and Story Centre in Great Missenden, in England, you can find out more about his life, dress up as characters from his books, and start thinking of ideas for your own stories.

Index